Festiniog
in the Fifties

Vic Mitchell and Allan Garraway

MP Middleton Press

*Front Cover: Having completed one of its first journeys in the revival era, **Prince** stands unattended outside the harbour offices in August 1955. (V.Mitchell)*

*Back cover upper: **Prince** waits to depart from Harbour station in July 1957. (P.Q.Treloar)*

*Back cover lower: On the town side of Harbour station stands **Prince** in September 1958 on the line that once connected the Festiniog Railway to the Welsh Highland. The track had last been used commercially in 1942, to take slates to a ship in the harbour. (N.F.Gurley)*

Published March 1996
Reprinted September 2013

ISBN 978 1 873793 68 8

© Middleton Press, 1996

Design Deborah Esher
Typesetting Barbara Mitchell

Published by
> *Middleton Press*
> *Easebourne Lane*
> *Midhurst*
> *West Sussex*
> *GU29 9AZ*
Tel: 01730 813169
Fax: 01730 812601
Email: info@middletonpress.co.uk
www.middletonpress.co.uk

Printed in the United Kingdom by IJ Graphics, Guildford, Surrey. GU2 9XW

CONTENTS

AUTHORS' NOTES

A childhood love affair with the 2ft gauge steam railway at Hampton Waterworks coupled with a picture of a double engine on the Festiniog Railway led to an ambition to visit the latter line, but sadly it closed before this could be fulfilled.

The Talyllyn Railway was operated by volunteers from May 1951 and in the following month I went with a friend (Alan French) to work on the permanent way. We replaced the rotten keys in the common chairs at rail ends on the unfishplated track above Dolgoch.

This first visit to Wales enabled me to visit the FR, walk down the top half of the line and see the other remains. Deeply impressed by the scale of the civil and mechanical engineering and already aware of its historical importance, it seemed obvious that this was the railway that should be saved.

Although both working on the Talyllyn Railway in the summer, your authors first met on 8th September 1951 at a meeting called in Bristol by enterprising teenager Leonard Heath-Humphreys. It was then that the Festiniog Railway Society was formed. As a student in London for most of the 1950s, I was able to be involved in the development of the society and was a director of FRS Ltd for its first nine years; and living in Wales from 1959 to 1962 enabled me to experience almost every aspect of the operation of the FR and to meet most of the photographers who have contributed to this album.

Subsequently, distance from the line precluded great involvement, but the founding of Middleton Press in 1981 has given an opportunity to develop further my general railway interest. It is particularly pleasing that the sales of our albums have brought financial benefit to so many private railways, not least the one that was thought to be so worth rescuing in 1951.

Vic Mitchell
Midhurst, West Sussex
February 1996

With Father having served his apprenticeship at Stratford Works and spent all his life with steam locomotives it was natural that I developed a similar interest from an early age, which gave me some rare and useful experiences.

The introduction of the then new Britannias to the Eastern Region in 1951 brought about a meeting with Bill Harvey (shedmaster at Norwich) which was to subsequently radically change my career. Over lunch, Bill, somewhat hesitatingly mentioned that he was planning to spend a week in July working in the Talyllyn Railway's workshops; I said that I had also recently joined this Society and agreed to join him.

Arriving by motorcycle on the Sunday, we introduced ourselves to Pendre Works (no trains and only emergency work on Sundays) and went on to look at the TR stations. Then we went north to see the Festiniog. Finding it a well engineered line, with heavy chaired track, we both felt that this was the railway we should be working on.

Shortly afterwards a letter appeared in the railway press concerning a meeting at Bristol to consider the possibility of reviving the FR. It was almost three years before Alan Pegler signed the cheques to obtain control of the FR Company. I endeavoured to lead the practical work while living in London, but realised that the FR needed someone full time. The announcement of the Modernisation Plan on BR indicated great changes which would include removing my beloved steam locomotives, so I offered my services full time to the FR Board. On 3rd June 1955 I became full time manager and engineer, general manager from 1958.

I lived "above the shop" at Harbour Station and had challenging tasks of great diversity, ranging from matters mechanical to sceptical Welshmen and from civil engineering to that new hitherto-unknown species, the "railway volunteer".

Those exciting and difficult years are described in more detail in Garraway Father and Son (Middleton Press); here follows a selection of photographs to further illustrate parts of that book.

Allan Garraway
Boat of Garten, Inverness-shire
February 1996

ACKNOWLEDGEMENTS

We have received an immense amount of help from many of the photographers mentioned in the captions; for this we are extremely grateful. Thanks also go to J.C.Gillham for use of his map, gradient profile, and plans drawn at that time. The FR chronology, which has been compiled by FRS members under the guidance of J.Hewitt, has been of great help. Appreciation is also recorded for the comments on the text from A.Ll.Lambert. The support of our wives is greatly valued, in particular Moyra Garraway, well known in all FR circles, for her own inimitable input to the railway.

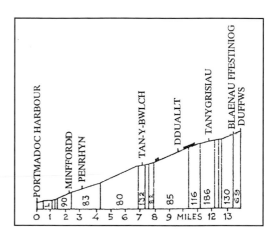

INTRODUCTION

Why did the Festiniog Railway have only one "F"? Why did it attract so many people concerned that it should be resuscitated? (This term was used in the 1950s, as the railway was too derelict and decayed for "preservation").

If you know the answers to these questions, then you could omit reading the next three paragraphs.

Strenuous efforts were made by nineteenth century governments to anglicise Wales so, when the Act of Parliament for the construction of the railway was drafted in 1832, the legislators used only one "F". The legally correct spelling was used throughout the fifties, despite the confusion and local opposition.

The advent of World War II forced withdrawal of passenger services on 15th September 1939, the final train for quarrymen running on the next day. A thrice-weekly slate train continued until 1st August 1946. After this date the line assumed the style of an ageing and declining form of "Sleeping Beauty".

Now we consider some of the features of the FR that appealed to potential resuscitators. Of great historical significance (opening in 1836), the line was the first public narrow gauge railway to use steam locomotives (from 1863) and the first railway of any gauge in Britain to use bogie coaches regularly (from 1873). The FR attained its greatest fame through its development of Robert Fairlie's patents for articulated and double ended engines which, among other important innovations, attracted several international delegations and prominent engineers in the 1870s. Images of the FR could still be seen all over the world in the 1950s but the pioneer was suffering a long and painful death.

The struggle to breath life back into this dormant ancestor of so many narrow gauge lines began in the late 1940s and involved numerous people and organisations.

The accompanying diagram was produced in 1979 by Dan Wilson in an attempt to clarify the complex events that led to the acquisition of control of the old company by Alan Pegler in June 1954.

With the support of a small staff and many FRS members, passenger services were restarted from Portmadoc as follows:

To		
	Boston Lodge	23 July 1955
	Minffordd	19 May 1956
	Penrhyn	20 April 1957
	Tan-y-bwlch	5 April 1958

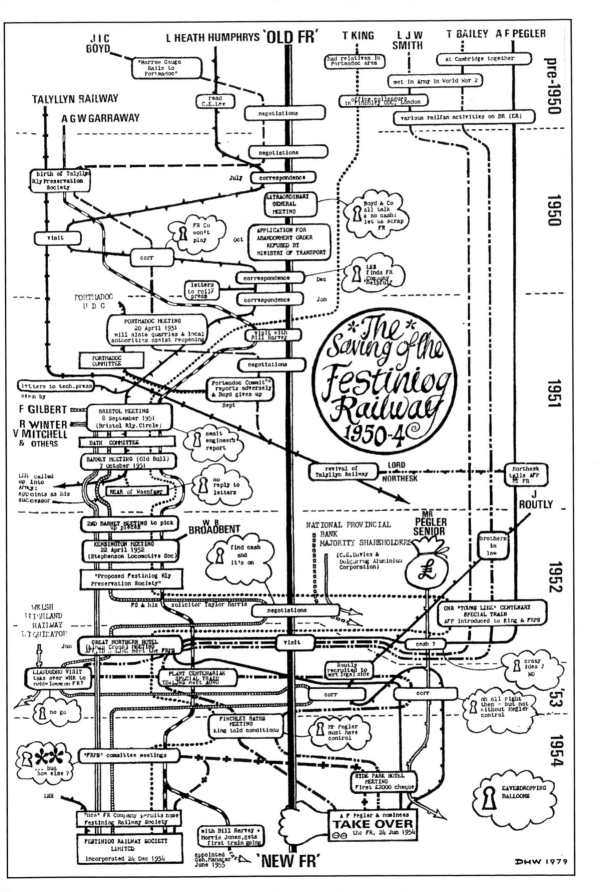

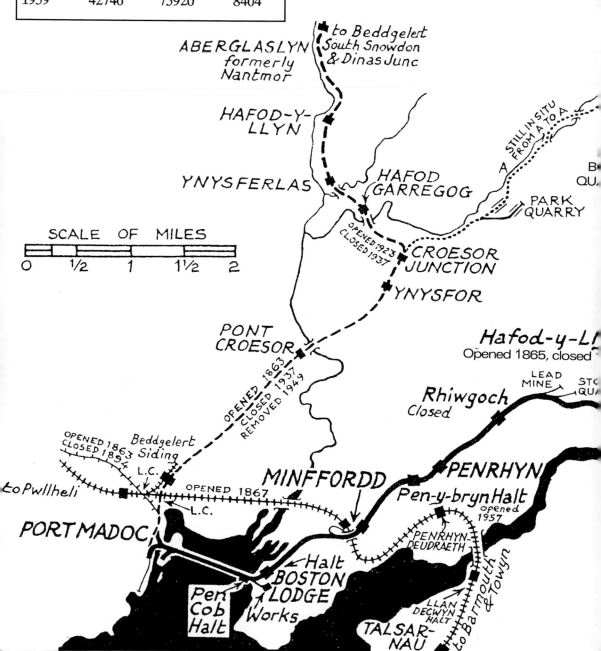

Year	Bookings	Journeys	Revenue £
1955	11530	21786	440
1956	20799	38671	1655
1957	28838	53557	2950
1958	32880	60128	6632
1959	42746	75920	8404

The FESTINIOG RAILWAY,
showing maximum track layout at stations
and at interchange points with 4'-8½" railways.

—— TRACKS STILL IN SITU IN 1957.
---- TRACKS LIFTED BEFORE 1957.

to Beddgelert
South Snowdon
& Dinas Junc

ABERGLASLYN
formerly
Nantmor

HAFOD-Y-
LLYN

STILL IN SITU
FROM A TO A

A

B
QU.

YNYSFERLAS

HAFOD
GARREGOG

PARK
QUARRY

OPENED 1923
CLOSED 1937

CROESOR
JUNCTION

YNYSFOR

SCALE OF MILES

0   ½   1   1½   2

PONT
CROESOR

Hafod-y-Ll
Opened 1865, closed

LEAD
MINE

ST(
QU.

Rhiwgoch
Closed

OPENED 1863
CLOSED 1937
REMOVED 1949

OPENED 1863
CLOSED 1894

Beddgelert
Siding
L.C.

PENRHYN

MINFFORDD

Pen-y-bryn Halt
opened
1957

to Pwllheli

OPENED 1867

L.C.

PENRHYN-
DEUDRAETH

PORT MADOC

Halt
BOSTON
LODGE
Works

Pen
Cob
Halt

LLAN
DECWYN
HALT

to Barmouth
& Towyn

TALSAR-
NAU

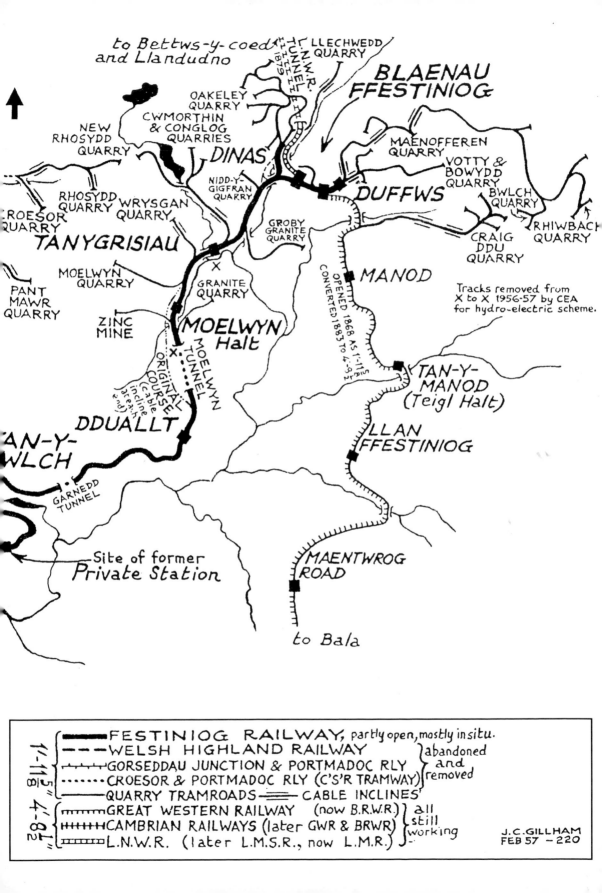

FESTINIOG RAILWAY COMPANY
TRAIN SERVICE

PORTMADOC (Harbour) and BOSTON LODGE (for Port Meirion).

PORTMADOC Dep.

x

10.30, 11.30 a.m., 1.30, 2.30, 3.30, 4.30, 5.30 p.m.

BOSTON LODGE Dep.

11.00 a.m., 12 noon, 3.00, 4.00, 5.00, 6.00 p.m.

X. Runs when required.

FARE 1/- Return. 8d. Single.

(CHILDREN UNDER 14 HALF PRICE).

The Festiniog Railway was the prototype of narrow gauge railways throughout the world. It was opened in 1836, and steam traction was introduced in 1863, with the locomotives "PRINCE" and "PRINCESS." The passenger Service was suspended in 1939 and the line closed in 1946.

The control of the shares of the Company was obtained by a railway enthusiast in 1954, and a new Board of Directors formed. Railway enthusiasts are supporting the Railway Company financially through the Festiniog Railway Society, and nearly all the work done in restoring the line has been done by voluntary effort. Your patronage and support will aid the railway to reopen further stretches through glorious scenery, in following years.

The original locomotive "PRINCE" has been reconditioned and is once more hauling trains.

A. G. W. GARRAWAY, Manager.

1955

Printed by Walker & Sons, Chester House, Dolgelley. Telephone No. 188.

FESTINIOG RAILWAY COMPANY

TIME TABLE

SATURDAY, 19th MAY TO SATURDAY, 22nd SEPTEMBER INCLUSIVE, WEEK-DAYS ONLY
ALSO SUNDAY, 20th MAY AND SUNDAY, 5th AUGUST

UP TRAINS		X	X				
Portmadoc	......	11.00	12.00	2.00	3.00	4.00	5.00
Pen Cob Halt	......	A	A	A	A	A	A
Boston Lodge	......	11.07	11.07	2.07	3.07	4.07	5.07
Minffordd	......	11.14	12.14	2.14	3.14	4.14	5.14

DOWN TRAINS		X	X				
Minffordd	......	11.30	12.30	2.30	3.30	4.35	5.30
Boston Lodge	......	11.37	12.37	2.37	3.37	4.42	5.37
Pen Cob Halt	......	A	A	A	A	A	A
Portmadoc	......	11.44	12.44	2.44	3.44	4.49	5.44

NOTES

A. Passengers wishing to alight at Pen Cob Halt (for the Beach) must advise the guard at Minffordd or Portmadoc. Passengers wishing to join the train must signal the driver to stop.

X   Runs 16th July to 8th September only, NOT Sunday, August 5th.

Special trains for parties at other times by prior arrangement.

All enquiries should be addressed to :—

THE MANAGER,
FESTINIOG RAILWAY COMPANY,
PORTMADOC,
CAERNS.   A. G. W. GARRAWAY, *Manager.*

T. STEPHENSON & SONS LTD., PRINTERS, PRESCOT, LANCS.

FESTINIOG RAILWAY COMPANY

1957

TIME TABLE

WEEK DAYS, 5th JUNE—28th SEPTEMBER.
ALSO WHIT SUNDAY AND AUGUST SUNDAY

UP TRAINS							
	A	A					B
Portmadoc	11.00	12.00	2.00	3.00	4.00	5.00	7.30
Minffordd	11.12	12.12	2.12	3.12	4.12	5.12	7.42
Penrhyndeudraeth	11.20	12.20	2.20	3.20	4.20	5.20	7.50
Tan-y-Bwlch							
Dduallt		Service temporarily suspended					
Tan-y-Grisiau							
Blaenau Ffestiniog							

DOWN TRAINS							
	A	A					B
Blaenau Ffestiniog							
Tan-y-Grisiau		Service temporarily suspended					
Dduallt							
Tan-y-Bwlch							
Penrhyndeudraeth	11.30	12.30	2.30	3.30	4.30	5.30	8.00
Minffordd	11.38	12.38	2.38	3.38	4.38	5.38	8.08
Portmadoc	11.50	12.50	2.50	3.50	4.50	5.50	8.20

A. Week-days only, 15th July—7th September, also Whit Monday.

B. Tuesdays, Wednesdays, Thursdays, and Saturdays, 16th July—7th September.
Also Whit Saturday and Whit Monday.

All trains call at Pen Cob, Boston Lodge and Pen-y-Bryn halts by request.

All enquiries should be addressed to :—

The Manager, Festiniog Railway Company, Portmadoc, Caerns.

Tel. Portmadoc 2340   A. G. W. GARRAWAY, *Manager*

T. STEPHENSON & SONS LTD., PRINTERS, PRESCOT, LANCS.

FESTINIOG RAILWAY COMPANY

TIME TABLE - 1958

WEEKDAYS ONLY, 24th MAY-27th SEPTEMBER, also 5th and 7th APRIL
SUNDAYS, 6th APRIL, 25th MAY and 3rd AUGUST
WEDNESDAYS ONLY, 9th APRIL-21st MAY and 1st-22nd OCTOBER—(See Note A)

(Photo by courtesy of the English Electric Co. Ltd.)

	PWLLHELI	dep.	9S25	9E55	12.45			
	PORTMADOC (W)	arr.	9S56	10E23	1.14			
	BARMOUTH	dep.		9.25	12.20	2S40	3E45	
	MINFFORDD	arr.		10.15	1.12	3S21dd	4E36	
	PORTMADOC (W)	arr.			1.16	3S26		
				B				C
0	PORTMADOC (Harbour)	dep.		10.40	2.30		4.30	7.30
$\frac{3}{4}$	PEN COB (Halt)	,,		dd	dd		dd	....
1	BOSTON LODGE (Halt)	,,		dd	dd		dd	dd
$2\frac{1}{4}$	MINFFORDD (for B.R. (W))	,,		10.52	2.42		4.42	dd
3	PEN-Y-BRYN (Halt)	,,		dd	dd		dd	....
$3\frac{1}{4}$	PENRHYN	,,		10.58	2.48		4.48	dd
$7\frac{1}{2}$	TAN-Y-BWLCH	arr.		11.25	3.15		5.15	8.10
9	DDUALLT	} Service temporarily suspended						
12	TAN-Y-GRISIAU	} Service temporarily suspended						
$13\frac{1}{4}$	BLAENAU FFESTINIOG	} Service temporarily suspended						
0	BLAENAU FFESTINIOG	} Service temporarily suspended						
$1\frac{1}{4}$	TAN-Y-GRISIAU	} Service temporarily suspended						
$4\frac{1}{4}$	DDUALLT	} Service temporarily suspended		B				C
$5\frac{3}{4}$	TAN-Y-BWLCH	dep.		11.45	3.30		5.30	8.40
10	PENRHYN	,,		12.12	3.57		5.57	dd
$10\frac{1}{4}$	PEN-Y-BRYN (Halt)	,,		dd	dd		dd	....
11	MINFFORDD (for B.R. (W))	,,		12.18	4.03		6.03	dd
$12\frac{1}{4}$	BOSTON LODGE (Halt)	,,		dd	dd		dd	dd
$12\frac{1}{2}$	PEN COB (Halt)	,,		dd	dd		dd	....
$13\frac{1}{4}$	PORTMADOC (Harbour)	arr.		12.30	4.15		6.15	9.20
	PORTMADOC (W)	dep.		1.17	4.35			
	MINFFORDD	dep.		1.22	4.40		6.08	
	BARMOUTH	arr.		2.12	5.27		6.57	
	MINFFORDD	dep.			4E31		6.17	
	PORTMADOC (W)	dep.		1.20	4E40	4S32	6.20	
	PWLLHELI	arr.		1.55	5E20	5S05	7.00	

Western Region times shown apply 9th June-13th September, week-days only.

A. On Wednesdays only, 9th April-21st May and 1st-22nd October, the 3-30 train will leave Tan-y-Bwlch at 3.45 and run 15 minutes later throughout. The 4.30 from Portmadoc and 5-30 from Tan-y-Bwlch will not run.

B. Runs 30th June-13th September, week-days only, also Easter Monday, 7th April.

C. Runs Tuesday, Wednesday, Thursday and Saturday only, 8th July-6th September, also Whit Saturday and Monday, May 24th and 26th.

Trains marked B and C may also run on other days by prior arrangement.

E. Except Saturdays. S. Saturdays only.

dd Calls when required to set down on notice to the Guard at previous stopping station; passengers wishing to join should give the necessary hand signal to the Driver.

T. STEPHENSON & SONS LTD., PRINTERS, PRESCOT, LANCS.

1. Rolling Stock

LOCOMOTIVES

Only four engines were functional in the fifties, though seldom all four simultaneously. They have been pictured in fine condition in many books and also occasionally elsewhere in this volume. They are illustrated here in less well known circumstances.

1.   The Simplex was one of hundreds made for use behind the lines in World War I. The pole behind the driver was one of four stanchions which were threaded to allow the roof height to be adjusted according to the intensity of shellfire. It was being prepared on 7th December 1954 for another tree-pulling trip, hence the chains. Later No. 7 van was renumbered 1. (F.Boughey)

2.   In early days there was no hostel accommodation, but a few slept on bunks in a room at the Harbour Station, usually eating across the road with Mrs May Jones. When early starts were needed, the fireman sometimes lit the fire while still in his pyjamas, leaving the engine to warm up while he washed and had his breakfast. This is a July 1957 view of *Prince*. (A.G.W.Garraway)

3. Both the FR "tractors", as they were so called between the wars, had petrol engines and were thus expensive to run. *Moelwyn* is being examined for conversion to diesel at Easter 1956 in Boston Lodge Yard, before being turned to face downhill. (A.G.W.Garraway)

4. *Taliesin* was the first double engine to be put back into traffic and is seen in grey primer on 30th March 1957 on the occasion of the Festiniog Railway Society's AGM. (D.W.Ronald)

COACHES

Rather than repeat classic side views in this album, we show some of the interior changes that took place in the fifties. Some of these innovative features were to herald a new era in narrow gauge coach design. The numbers quoted are those used by the new management, although the old numbers continued in use for a brief period.

5. When no. 17 was restored to traffic in 1956, its first class was cleaned up and given "new" seat cushions, from old buses. David Ronald embroidered antimacassars, causing eyebrows to be raised in the ladies shop where he bought yards of lace in June 1958.
(A.G.W.Garraway)

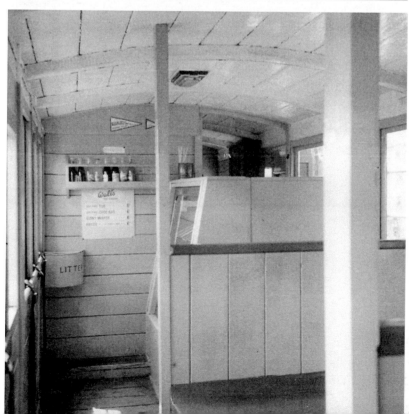

6. For the 1956 season, with trains running to Minffordd, no. 11 brake third was turned to give a brake at each end of the train (see picture no. 41). For 1957 it ran van to van with no. 12, the vacuum pipes being moved, fall plates and handrails provided so that it was possible to pass from van to van. At the same time a small counter was put into no. 12 instead of the longitudinal seating, and a corridor made through from the van to facilitate dealing with passengers from unstaffed halts. The signs in June 1958 announced that ice creams and minerals were available at 6d each. (A.G.W.Garraway)

7.   From the earliest days of revival there had been dreams of building a real observation car to go on the end of the train. The rear of no. 11 offered a relatively simple and cheap conversion using windows and seating from Mersey Railway coaches then being scrapped. This provided two corridor coaches through which the guard could go to check tickets, collect supplementary fares etc. all giving useful revenue as well as experience before superior new vehicles could be built. (A.G.W.Garraway)

8.   Turning the camera 180 degrees we see the unique observation end windows and the limited legroom available. Both photographs are from 1958, during which year a supplementary charge (one shilling) was made for travelling in the "Obs". (A.G.W.Garraway)

9.   The within was evident from without in June 1958. No. 2, a four-wheeled van, had origially been a quarrymens coach and had vacuum brakes. It had been in the joiners shop during closure (for repairs to one side) and was comparatively sound. So it was brought into the "active" part of the Works for overhaul to replace no. 1 van in passenger service. (A.G.W.Garraway)

2. The Welsh Highland Connection

A Light Railway Order had been granted in 1923 for a line to link the WHR and FR along the eastern edge of the town. Much of it used the existing route of the Croesor Railway in this vicinity and was still in situ in the 1950s.

10.   Two photographs from September 1950 confirm that track was still in place west of Harbour station. At the flour mill there was a shelter over a loop siding; parallel to it had been the WHR line which had crossed the GWR near the telephone pole. There had been a junction in the foreground, the line on the left being shown more fully in the next picture. (F.Boughey)

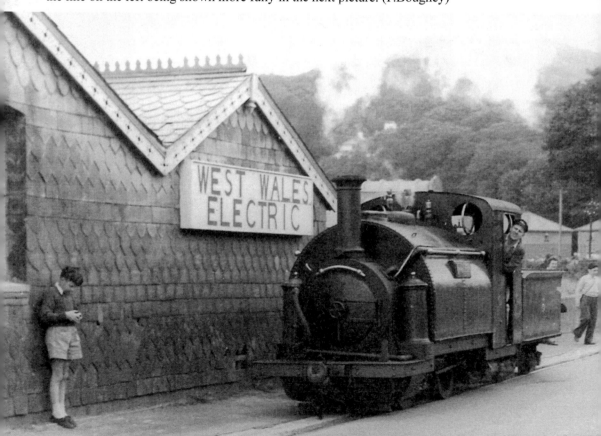

→ 11. This line had once been part of the Gorseddau Junction & Portmadoc Railway but for many decades had only carried slate from the FR to the slate works on the left. See picture no. 53 in *Branch Lines to Portmadoc 1923-46* and the adjacent map. (F.Boughey)

↓ 12. The Festiniog line across the Britannia Bridge to the slate wharves and Welsh Highland line had remained, and in September 1958 *Prince* went across the bridge, leaving the rail bolsters onto which the rails could be loaded after they had been lifted. The line had been used in 1954 by the Simplex when needing petrol from the filling station. (N.F.Gurley)

3. The Resuscitated Railway

PORTMADOC HARBOUR

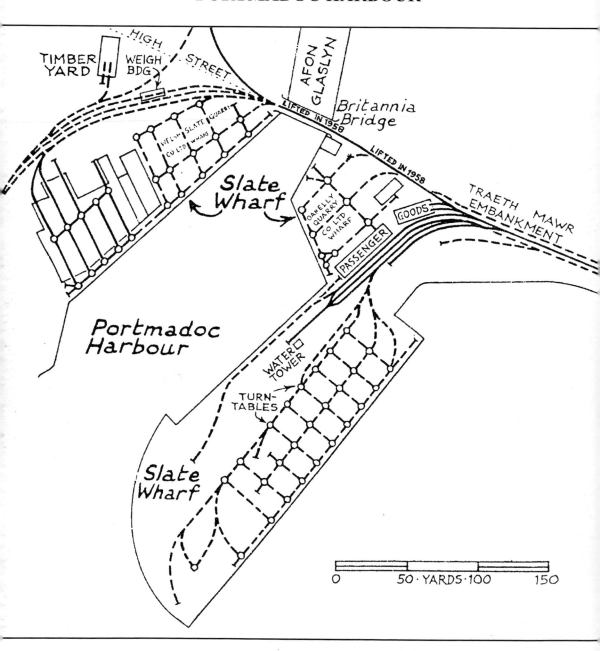

13. Harbour Station was recorded on 15th July 1951, as nature gradually took over. The passenger coaches had been taken to Boston Lodge during the war, where out of doors, they succumbed in similar manner. (A.G.W.Garraway)

14.   With all the strings of slate wagons, the one remaining iron horse dandy survived (just), it having been a coal wagon in the final years. Also photographed in 1950 is the Britannia Foundry, which was later to cast firebars for the FR. Note the wooden wagons nearby. (F.Boughey)

15.   In hindsight, this was one of the mistakes of those early days. When every penny was needed for rebuilding *Prince* and for new sleepers for the track, everything that had no possibility of further use was scrapped. The remains of the ex-WHR *Moel Tryfan* were considered beyond repair and joined the slate wagons to become washing machines. The trailing bogie did survive, and was used for the leading pony trucks for *Linda* and *Blanche*. The last movement of the hulk was captured on film on 2nd October 1954. (A.G.W.Garraway)

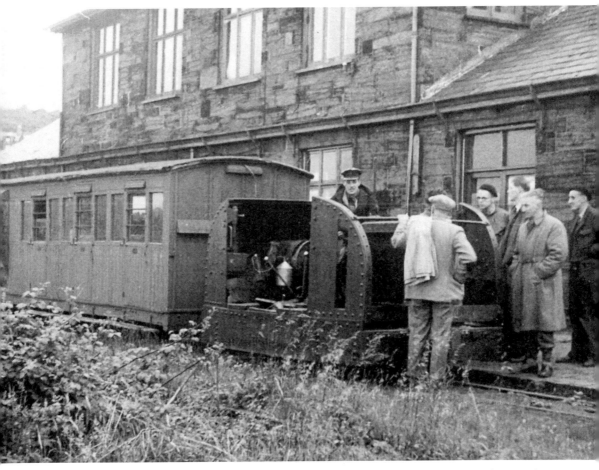

16. Coach no. 11 was used in the winter of 1954-55 to transport volunteer workers and as a mobile mess. The ducket was prone to hit bulging stone walls. The Simplex had lost its roof supports by now. (F.Boughey)

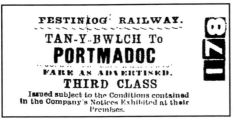

17.   This is the formation that worked most of the trains in that first short season, *Prince* with no. 23 and no. 12. The nameplate is a temporary wooden device. This and the next picture date from 3rd September 1955. (A.M.Davies)

18. The fireman checks that 90-year old *Prince* runs onto the three-way stub point safely. Close by are the remnants of the point indicator and the water tower. (A.M.Davies)

19. *Prince* is in works primer as it shunts wagons and a lifeless *Merddin Emrys* on 29th April 1956. The engine had been on show for the FRS AGM a month earlier. The next picture was taken a few minutes later. (F.Boughey)

20.   With relaying of the Harbour Station throat in progress, *Prince* takes a load of spoil and *Merddin Emrys* back to Boston Lodge. The former goods shed is in the background (left) and the Britannia Foundry is behind *Prince*. (F.Boughey)

21.   Water supply at the terminus was essential for the 1956 season and so the tank was replaced. It is seen on test on 13th May, three days before services commenced to Minffordd. (J.Halsall)

22.   *Taliesin* is coaled direct from the Cleminson six-wheeled iron coal wagon, only one of its end doors being visible. It is standing on the siding over which slate wagons once ran to South Snowdon Wharf, seen clearly in the next picture. (N.F.Gurley)

23.   The tapered coal stage is seen between *Taliesin* and the Cleminson wagon on 22nd August 1958 as a helicopter provides a contrasting form of transport. (A.G.W.Garraway)

24. *Taliesin* was not used on short trains if a small engine was available. This train is composed of nos. 11, 12 and two Victorian bogie coaches and has just passed the old "trident" signal post which had stood on The Cob since about 1929. The main arm had been restored for its original purpose. (N.F.Gurley)

25. Few photographs show *Moelwyn* facing uphill. One of the advantages of turning it was to facilitate sanding when running up hill. It seldom ran on the main line pre-war, normally being used for shunting. Until named at the end of 1956, it was known as the Baldwin or the Tractor. It is on its first job of work after the fitting of a Gardner 3LW diesel engine and is about to depart for Blaenau Ffestiniog on 5th August 1956. (F.Boughey)

26.   After opening to Tan-y-Bwlch in 1958, so many passengers were being left behind that three of the four-wheelers were cleaned up and, with no. 1 van, made into a relief train, known as the "Flea". The coaches' low ground clearance necessitated checks and a little work at some places to stop them grounding. See picture no. 91. (N.F.Gurley)

27.　　Taken a few minutes after the cover picture, *Prince* returns from Britannia Bridge with rails recovered from the road. All trace of this piece of history has vanished. (N.F.Gurley)

28.　　Turning to the left we see the stub of the connection once used by WHR trains. The goods shed was fairly sound and *Moelwyn* is about to push the unique hearse and the sole remaining wooden slate wagon into it. The latter were known as bobbin wagons, owing to the type of cast spacers between the bars. (N.F.Gurley)

29.   Access to Harbour Station had always been from the platform, the one-time slate wharf behind being completely walled off. Use of the wharf for car parking was obtained, and thereafter access to the building, for staff and public, was made on the north side in 1960. Photographs of this side before the alteration are very rare; this one dates from September 1959. (M.Seymour)

1959 plan of proposed alterations, 2mm to 1ft.

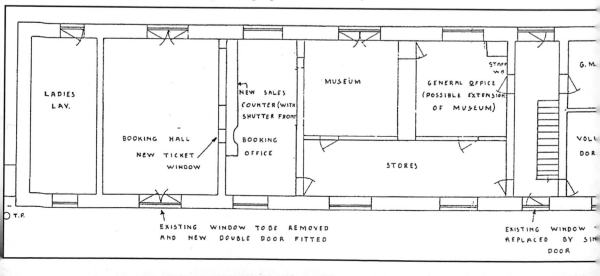

LADIES
LAV.

BOOKING   HALL

NEW   TICKET
WINDOW

NEW   SALES
COUNTER (WITH
SHUTTER FRONT

BOOKING
OFFICE

·MUSEUM·

STORES

STAFF
W B

GENERAL   OFFICE
(POSSIBLE EXTENSION
OF   MUSEUM)

G. M.

VOL.
DOR

T.P.

EXISTING   WINDOW   TO BE   REMOVED
AND   NEW   DOUBLE   DOOR   FITTED

EXISTING   WINDOW
REPLACED   BY   SIM
DOOR

➔ 30. The demolition of the gentlemens toilet at the south end of the building took place in the last month of 1959. This was to enable the road to be widened for the movement of heavy electrical equipment from ships to Trawsfynydd Nuclear Power Station. In the event, another wharf was used. (A.G.W.Garraway)

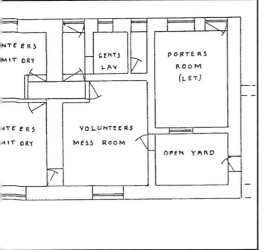

NTE ERS
MIT ORY

GENTS
LAY

PORTERS
ROOM
(LET)

NTE ERS
MIT ORY

VOLUNTEERS
MESS ROOM

OPEN YARD

BOSTON LODGE WORKS

31.   The locked gates on 1st April 1951 hid the rotting chaos inside, but the neglected stock outside gave a clue. Smoke rises from one of the cottages. (F.Boughey)

32.   Inside the yard on 13th September 1953 were the coaches of the last down train. Left to right are nos. 15, 19 and 21. Nos 15 and 16, built in 1872, were the first bogie coaches in regular use in Great Britain and were thus important items to be saved for posterity. (A.M.Davies)

33.   Just past the Works was the locomotive running shed. Photographed in 1950, the tracks were lost from sight under grass but they led to hidden treasures. (J.L.Bate)

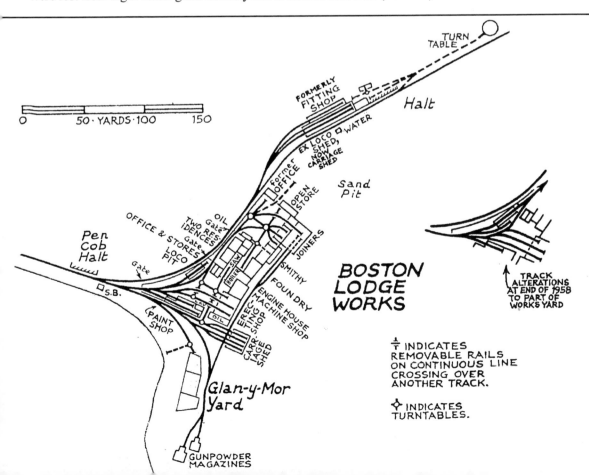

TURN TABLE

Halt

FORMERLY FITTING SHOP

EX LOCO SHED, NOW CARRIAGE SHED

WATER

Sand Pit

Former OFFICE

OPEN STORE

JOINERS

0   50 · YARDS · 100   150

OIL Gate

OFFICE & STORES

TWO RES IDENCES

Gate

LOCO PIT

SMITHY

FOUNDRY

ENGINE HOUSE

MACHINE SHOP

BOSTON LODGE WORKS

TRACK ALTERATIONS AT END OF 1958 TO PART OF WORKS YARD

Pen Cob Halt

Gate

S.B.

PAINT SHOP

OIL

ERECTING SHOP

BOILER

SAW

CARRIAGE SHED

⊥ INDICATES REMOVABLE RAILS ON CONTINUOUS LINE CROSSING OVER ANOTHER TRACK.

◇ INDICATES TURNTABLES.

Glan-y-Mor Yard

GUNPOWDER MAGAZINES

34.   Quietly rusting away outside Glan-y-Mor carriage shed in 1951 was iron coal wagon no. 18. Next to it was a slate wagon that had been boarded up for granite traffic. (F.Boughey)

35.   The Simplex is approaching the Works gates on 6th November 1954 with no. 10 prior to running the special train to Minffordd seen in picture no. 59. On 21st September of that year, the first wheels had turned since 1946. (F.Boughey)

36. Pictured outside the Works gates on 4th December 1954 is the Simplex and no. 1 van. Behind the latter is a World War "pill box" intended for the defence of the district. It would not have withstood much, judging by the ease with which it was dismantled in the next year. The shelter on the left housed point levers; it had earlier had a glazed front to form a conventional signal box. (F.Boughey coll.)

37. New levers (right) were installed at Easter 1955; cutting the recess for the angle crank is in progress. The clearance between the pill box and passenger trains was considered insufficient. Pen Cob Halt was opened here in May 1956 to serve what was then a pleasant area of beach. (F.Boughey coll.)

38.   A new boiler awaited *Prince* when the FR was taken over and so reassembly was one of the first tasks. Cape Asbestos donated some of their blue asbestos seen here soon after application in June 1955. All traces of it has long gone. (A.G.W.Garraway)

39.   *Prince* was filled with water for the first time on 28th July 1955, using a hose from the toll gate.
The Works had its own water supply but no mains electricity prior to 1955. (A.G.W.Garraway)

40.   Work had to go on in all weathers and so the lack of a roof on the Simplex was not appreciated as it came round the curve outside the works on 8th January 1956. (F.Boughey)

41.   As explained earlier, coach no. 11 was turned. This difficult task was undertaken at Easter 1956 in Glan-y Mor Yard by putting the van end on a wagon turntable and sliding the other end on rails and sleepers. (F.Boughey)

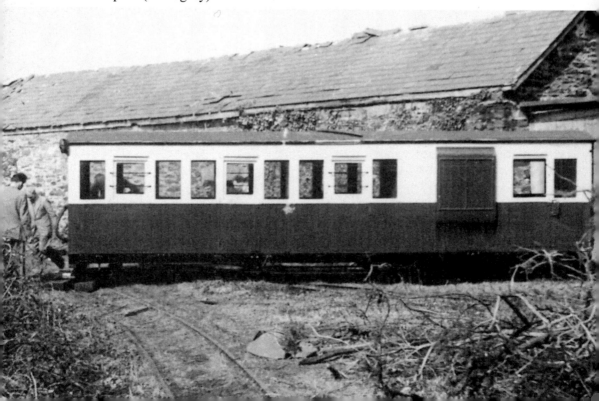

42.   Prior to closure, daily locomotive servicing had been undertaken at the shed seen in picture
no. 33. A new pit was constructed in the main or west yard in April 1956. (A.G.W.Garraway)

43.   Top or east yard was the resting place for *Palmerston* in 1956. The engine had stood there for many years to provide power for the steam hammer. (F.Boughey)

44.   The Crossley hot-bulb diesel engine drove the line shafting for the machines. Starting the engine got the circulation going on a cold winter morning - there was no heating in the early days. Note the flare for lighting. There was no electricity until early in 1955 when a limited single phase supply was brought in. The cab belongs to *Prince*. (F.Boughey)

45. The top bogie of *Taliesin* was recorded along with the aged belt drives to various machines. Double engines have top and bottom bogies, the terms relating to the gradient of the line. This and the next two photographs were taken in August 1956. (A.G.W.Garraway)

46.   Oh bother!! During shunting, when the train stopped, the door and part of the side just slid to the ground. Fred Boughey holds it for the photograph. No. 12 was scrapped in 1958. (A.G.W.Garraway)

47.   A length of the original wrought-iron fishbelly rail on stone blocks was discovered in August 1956, when digging out the old wagon shop floor in the top yard. (F.Boughey)

48.   Glan-y-Mor yard was pictured in September 1958 with the ex-Harrogate Gasworks Peckett 0-6-0ST, which some hoped would resolve the chronic locomotive shortage; it never ran on the FR due to its weight and to the wheelbase being too long for the sharpest curves. The long shed and bottom yard are at the top of the picture. (D.W.Ronald)

49.   *Moelwyn*, which had proved a very useful engine but terribly lively in its riding, was extended at the front and given a pony truck. This cured the problem and gave a useful space for carrying tools etc. Here it is with the ex-Lynton & Barnstaple Railway underframe going to Garnedd Tunnel to test clearances on 14th May 1959, only four days after the frame had arrived from Devon. See pictures 118 to 120, (A.G.W.Garraway)

50.   Boston Lodge main yard was photographed in June 1959 with a skeletal *Merddin Emrys*, its new tanks on slate wagons (fabricated by John Summers of Shotton), coupled to *Taliesin* and *Prince*. *Moelwyn* is shunting all three. (A.G.W.Garraway)

51.   This panorama includes Boston Lodge Yard, with the pattern shop roof and iron foundry chimney in the foreground, the stores and office beyond, the long shed to the left and the Cob stretchng to Harbour Station. The corrugated iron fence was demolished in August 1958. (N.F.Gurley)

52.   The boiler for *Merddin Emrys* was overhauled by Vulcan Foundry and is seen under steam test on the 21st August 1959. It was to be almost another two years before the overhaul of the rest of the engine was completed and it entered traffic. (A.G.W.Garraway)

53. *Prince* with a train of ex-WHR rails and *Taliesin* with nos. 22 and 23 pose outside the Works. There was over 4ins of super elevation on this curve at that time. Note the firewood on the left and the steps taking the footpath that passes over the Cob down onto the road. Owing to the danger of the then very narrow road, many people chose to walk through the Works or along the FR track. (N.F.Gurley)

BOSTON LODGE HALT

54.   The first track clearance was done by a party from St. Paul's School with Mike Elvy, who worked up from Boston Lodge in a very wet week. The results of their efforts were photographed on 5th September 1954. (A.G.W.Garraway)

55.　　Just above Boston Lodge Halt, a culvert had collapsed, leaving the track suspended. Before anything could move up the line the track had to be supported on timbers, but by Easter 1955 the culvert had been repaired, the ground filled in, and Rev. Timmy Phillips, who lived in the far railway house in the background provided some ballast to make it look very good. (A.G.W.Garraway)

56.   Near the house was the disused turntable. This and its counterpart at Glan-y-Pwll had been out of use since 1923. It could have been useful if it had been within any of the siding complexes. Rev. Phillips built a garage on it so that he could drive in forwards, turn the entire garage, and then drive out forwards down the narrow access road. (F.Boughey)

57.　　On 23rd July 1955, a train service started between Portmadoc and Boston Lodge, using the Simplex and coaches 23 and 12. *Prince* took over the service on 2nd August and was adorned with flags for the occasion. The total revenue for the first season was £440. (F.Boughey)

58.　　In 1957, Rhiw Plas bridge carried the main A497 road over the railway. Narrow and totally inadequate for modern traffic, particularly the heavy equipment coming in by sea to go to the new nuclear power station at Trawsfynydd, it was rebuilt in 1960. (A.G.W.Garraway)

MINFFORDD

59.　　On 6th November 1954, a special train was run to Minffordd for directors and guests. As the loop and top points had not been cleared, running round had to be by hand shunting on the bottom points, and the wet grass made adhesion difficult anyway. Boiling of the coolant was not uncommon until satisfactory fan belts were obtained. (F.Boughey)

60.　　The wooden shelter on Minffordd down platform was in a very poor condition and was too close to the track. *Prince* and a chain soon pulled it down for firewood on 5th May 1956. Its replacement was in hand 40 years later. (P.J.G.Ransom)

61.   *Taliesin* was overhauled in 1956 and worked her first full day on 5th September. She is seen two weeks later on trial after further adjustments. (K.Cribb)

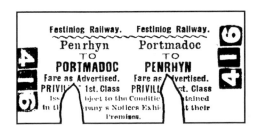

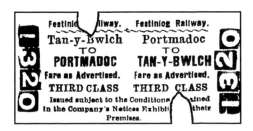

62.   The track was still grass covered when *Taliesin* was recorded in July 1958 with a train of all seven restored bogie coaches from Tan-y-Bwlch. The penultimate coach is no. 22 which was rushed into service partly painted and minus some doors. At this time coaches were green and cream with red ends. (N.F.Gurley)

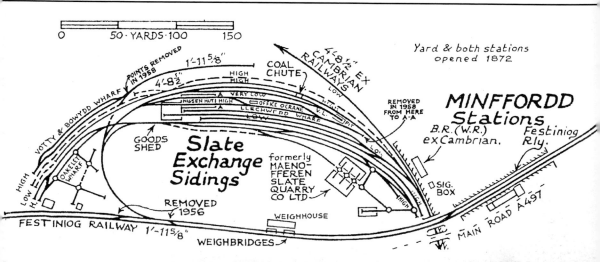

0   50 · YARDS · 100   150

Yard & both stations opened 1872

POINTS REMOVED IN 1958
1'-11⅝"
4'-8½"
HIGH HIGH
VERY LOW
N16.5EN HUT HIGH
LLECHWEDD WHARF
OFFICE O'CRANE V.L.
LOW
A-A

COAL CHUTE
4'8½" EX CAMBRIAN RAILWAYS
LOW

REMOVED IN 1958 FROM HERE TO A-A

MINFFORDD
Stations
B.R.(W.R.)   Festiniog
ex Cambrian.   Rly.

VOTTY & BOWYDD WHARF
HIGH
OAKELEY WHARF
LOW
H.L.

GOODS SHED

Slate Exchange Sidings

formerly MAENO-FFEREN SLATE QUARRY CO LTD

REMOVED 1956

SIG. BOX

HIGH

FESTINIOG RAILWAY 1'-11⅝"

WEIGHHOUSE

WEIGHBRIDGES

MAIN ROAD A497

63.	An ailing *Taliesin*, working on only one bogie is assisted by the Simplex on the 4.30pm from Portmadoc on 20th August 1958. Note the bell on the Simplex, originally on *Little Wonder*, the first Fairlie of 1869. (F.Boughey coll.)

64.	*Taliesin* is taking coal empties to Minffordd Yard on 10th July 1959. She will run round, pick up no. 2 van and return to Boston Lodge, the wagons being gravitated into the yard. (J.L.Alexander)

MINFFORDD YARD

65.   A couple of slate wagons, a van, and the Cleminson six-wheel wagon, with the corrugated roof added for carrying flour, stood at the long siding buffer stops during the closure period. (F.Boughey)

66.   FR wagons were used by slate merchants for loading slates onto BR wagons. Supplies were brought by road from the quarries and stacked on the right and in sheds out of view in this 1954 photograph. The main line station in the distance was still manned. (A.G.W.Garraway)

67.   Clearance of the "sunken road" at Minffordd Yard took place in September 1955. The chute made coal transhipment from BR wagons much easier. Note gunpowder vans (left) waiting to go to Cooke's Explosives factory at Penrhyndeudracth. (A.G.W.Garraway)

68.   An ex-GWR 2200 class 0-6-0 shunts wagons in Minffordd Yard in about 1959. Maenofferen Slate Quarry Company's slate shed is on the left. The siding on the right served the coal chute. (F.Boughey)

Attractive Afternoon Outing

TO

TAN-Y-BWLCH

(via Minffordd)

AND

THE FESTINIOG LIGHT RAILWAY

(Britain's Oldest Public Narrow Gauge Railway)

15th June to 26th September, 1959

(Saturdays Excepted)

FROM	Depart	Return Fare Second Class	FROM	Depart	Return Fare Second Class
	p.m.	s. d.		p.m.	s. d.
BARMOUTH	3 45	5/9	PWLLHELI	4 5	5/6
DYFFRYN ARDUDWY ...	3 57	5/-	ABERERCH	4 10	5/3
LL & PENSARN	4 5	4/9	PENYCHAIN	4 13	5/-
HARLECH	4 13	4/6	CRICCIETH	4 24	4/6
MINFFORDD arr.	4 31	—	MINFFORDD arr.	4 42	—

Children under Three years of age, Free; Three and under Fourteen years of age, Half-fare.

FESTINIOG RAILWAY

			p.m.
MINFFORDD ... ... dep.			4 42
TAN-Y-BWLCH ... ... arr.			5 15
TAN-Y-BWLCH ... ... dep.			5 30
MINFFORDD ... ... arr.			6 3

CONNECTING SERVICES ON RETURN JOURNEY.

		p.m.			p.m.
MINFFORDD ... ... dep.		6 11	MINFFORDD ... ... dep.		6 25
HARLECH ... ... arr.		6 34	CRICCIETH ... ... arr.		6 40
LL. & PENSARN ... ... ,,		6 41	PENYCHAIN ... ... ,,		6 52
DYFFRYN ARDUDWY ... ... ,,		6 49	ABERERCH HALT ... ... ,,		6 55
BARMOUTH ... ... ,,		7 0	PWLLHELI ... ... ,,		7 2

PASSENGERS CHANGE AT MINFFORDD IN EACH DIRECTION

Further information will be supplied on application to the Stations or to Mr. O. VELTOM, District Traffic Superintendent, Oswestry (Telephone Oswestry 189, Extension 211); or Mr. E. FLAXMAN, Commercial Officer, Paddington Station, W.2.

Paddington Station, W.2.

March, 1959.

J. R. HAMMOND,

General Manager.

No. 21.

Printed in Great Britain by G. R. Griffith Ltd., Chester.

PENRHYN

69. This and the next picture show the Simplex on one of the six trips to the top end of the line in 1956. Local lads witness the event on 28th July. (A.M.Davies)

70. A train was a rare event here in 1956. The purpose of the trip was to collect materials from the Blaenau Ffestiniog area. Plans were considered for an automated crossing but have never been implemented. (A.M.Davies)

71. *Moelwyn* and no. 1 van stand on the siding points in the Autumn of 1956. Until closure the siding had received flour for the nearby bakery via Blaenau Ffestiniog. Note the wagon turntable which gave wagons access to the goods shed. (N.F.Gurley)

72. K.W.C.Grand, General Manager of BR Western Region, was coming to Wales to see the proposed Llyn Celyn scheme, which would cut the Bala - Blaenau Ffestiniog branch and its connection with Arenig Quarry. He had intimated a desire to see the FR as well. Great efforts were made to enable *Taliesin* and train to get to Penrhyn, from where the party went by road to Tan-y-Bwlch and *Moelwyn* took them to the tunnel. Clearance had to be done around Highgate Crossing on 11th November 1956. (A.G.W.Garraway)

73.   Before the test train entered the station, the wagons were shunted into the siding. *Taliesin* and train attracted much attention in the station; the residents above were not so pleased. (A.G.W.Garraway)

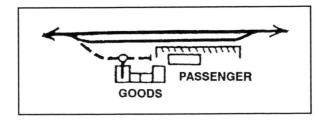

GOODS

PASSENGER

74.   Before the station could be used as a terminus for the 1957 season, a loop had to be laid.
This shows progress on 30th January of that year and that the siding and turntable had gone.
(A.G.W.Garraway)

75.   The informal reopening of the station was put on record on Easter Saturday, 20th April 1957. Some flags add to the occasion. (F.Boughey)

76.   A great effort was made in 1957 to complete clearance of the line to Tan-y-Bwlch and when Keith Catchpole had his party of Enfield schoolboys at work, *Prince* and no. 10 took them up the line. They returned to Penrhyn and then were atached to the front of the passcnger train, one of the rare occasions when no. 10 ran in such a train. (A.G.W.Garraway)

77.   A typical example of the growth which had taken place on the track in the couple of miles below Tan-y-Bwlch by 1954. (J.B.Snell)

78.   The first move towards the building of Tanygrisiau pumped storage scheme was the construction of an access road from Blaenau Ffestiniog down to the site, much of which, altered at the ends, is now the bypass. This cut the FR immediately above Stesion Fain, the old FR connecting station to the Conway Valley line. Before this cut took place, as many wagons as possible were collected from the quarries and then brought down to Minffordd. Simplex brought one massive train on 27th September 1955, here seen at Cei Mawr. (A.G.W.Garraway)

79.   One of the earliest quarrymens coach bodies had been in use as a permanent way hut at Llechwedd Coed, near Plas Tan-y-Bwlch. (Unknown)

80.   At first a way was hacked through to get a train to Blaenau Ffestniog, particularly to show the electricity authorities that trains could be run over the whole railway, which they had said was impossible. However much further effort was needed to complete the clearing before regular passenger trains could run, and here *Prince* is hauling out some of the large roots on a summer evening in July 1957. (A.G.W.Garraway)

81.　　Clearance of ivy from walls and cutting back brambles and gorse were less spectacular but necessary tasks undertaken in the summer of 1957. Even after this, regrowth was a problem and drivers often carried sickles or garden shears to cut back brambles threatening to hit them in the face. This is an evening relaxation for *Prince* after hauling passengers all day. (N.F.Gurley)

The tickets seen so far in this album are examples of those produced for the new management. Here follows samples of old stock that continued to be used in the 1950s.

82. At Hafod-y-Llyn a hole was discovered in the ground beside the track, the rock slab forming the culvert roof having collapsed. A concrete slab was cast and the hole filled in. The ladder was lowered into the chasm on 18th January 1958. (A.G.W.Garraway)

83. Immediately adjacent to the bridge over the road at Tan-y-Bwlch (just visible at top of photograph), the high dry stone wall on the outside of the curve showed signs of bulging. The culvert was extended with concrete pipes, and the area filled with spoil mostly from the widening of Rhiw Plas Bridge. This picture is from December 1959. (A.G.W.Garraway)

TAN-Y-BWLCH

84.   The goods shed and abandoned stock were photographed in September 1952, together with the chickens belonging to the occupants of the station house, former FR employees, Will and Bessie Jones. (F.Boughey)

85.   Pictured in 1954 is the original station building and the water tank. Will Jones had optimistically oiled the points since closure and throughout the 1950s. (F.Boughey)

86.   The Simplex, no. 17 coach and no. 1 van formed the third train to penetrate Moelwyn Tunnel since the closure. It was recorded outside the station house on 5th March 1955. (A.G.W.Garraway)

87.   Ian Smart restored this platelayers trolley, known as "Busta". Unsprung and very light, it had two speeds, described by one person as fast and very fast. It didn't have a lot of use; it couldn't carry anything, which was probably just as well! Bessie Jones watches from her front door in 1955. (F.Boughey)

88.   Previously seen in pictures 69 and 70, the Simplex shunts wagons on 28th July 1956, before proceeding to Blaenau to recover materials. (A.M.Davies)

89.   The old water tank had to be scrapped; the water was particularly acidic here. The replacement came from Laxfield, Suffolk and is seen arriving on 16th January 1958. (A.G.W.Garraway)

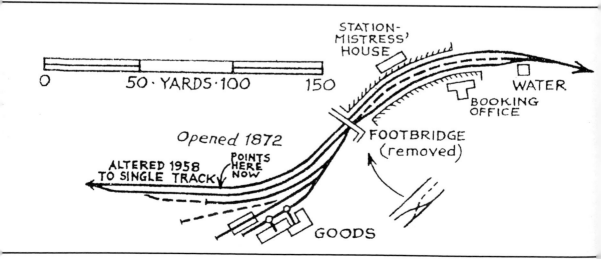

STATION-
MISTRESS'
HOUSE

0   50 · YARDS · 100   150   WATER

BOOKING
OFFICE

Opened 1872   FOOTBRIDGE
(removed)

ALTERED 1958   POINTS
TO SINGLE TRACK   HERE
NOW

GOODS

90. Regular service recommenced on 5th April 1958. *Taliesin* is seen with a short trial train a few days earlier. Fencing and platforms were way into the future. The Austin minicoach was hired by the London Area Group for weekend working parties in 1958. The Isetta bubble car was also used for the overnight journey. (N.F.Gurley)

91. The trial run of the "Flea" or "Flying Flea" was recorded on 4th August 1958. This relief train was seen previously in picture no. 26. Appropriately the coaches soon became known as the "Bug Boxes". Here are nos. 4, 5 and 6 with no. 1 van. (Alice V.Boughey)

92.　　Turf embedded rails in a wooded hollow on a beautiful hillside made a memorable finale for tourists enjoying this unique journey in the late 1950s. Thousands made a photographic record here. (A.M.Davies)

4. The Dormant Railway
DDUALLT

93.   Above Tan-y-Bwlch there was little other than the occasional gorse bush or rock obstructing the track. The Simplex passes Dduallt on 28th July 1956 on the journey seen earlier in pictures 69, 70 and 88. (A.M.Davies)

NORTH OF DDUALLT

94.   After the great clearance work of 1957, it was deemed feasible to take *Prince* and coaches with the workers to Tan-y-Bwlch on 6th September, and on 22nd *Prince* with no. 10 went through to Moelwyn Tunnel. Just for fun, the train went inside and this photograph was taken of the last steam to come from it. (A.G.W.Garraway)

95.　　Another excuse to take *Prince* to the mouth of Moelwyn Tunnel came on 6th December 1958 during a survey of locations for a promotional film. Nos. 11 and 12 formed the train. (A.G.W.Garraway)

96.　　Another unusual picture shows the top of one of the three ventilation shafts of the tunnel and the rear end of the FRS chairman, Bill Broadbent as he peers down the shaft. (A.G.W.Garraway)

97.   Only a few walkers have had the chance to see the track towards Tanygrisiau from above the north tunnel mouth. Tunnel Cottage is between the main line and the branch to Brooke's Quarry. The cottage had a Post Office letterbox set into its wall. Moelwyn Zinc Mine is on the left; its siding branches off beyond the cottage. (A.M.Davies)

98.   Looking at the north portal of the tunnel in August 1954, we have the opportunity of also seeing the Brooke's Quarry branch, unclear in the previous picture. (A.M .Davies)

99.   The junction (left) to Wrysgan Quarry, just below Tanygrisiau, is now virtually under the road to the Power Station. The waterfall and cottages at the bottom end of the new station are visible, and the embankment of the original line can be seen in the centre of this 1950 photograph. (A.M.Davies)

TANYGRISIAU

100.   The train seen in pictures 69,70, 88 and 93 on its way to Glan-y-Pwll shunted its wagons into the siding at Tanygrisiau, but then became derailed. Equipment to deal with such emergencies was always carried on these expeditions. (A.M.Davies)

101.   A second photograph here on 28th July 1956 shows children swarming over the train as the Simplex waits to propel the wagons up the line after they had been manhandled out of the siding. Of the cluster of buildings in the background, only the goods shed (second nearest the camera) survives. (A.M.Davies)

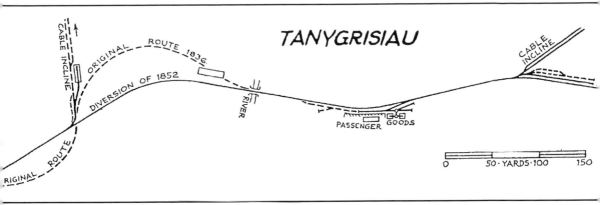

TANYGRISIAU

CABLE INCLINE

ORIGINAL ROUTE 1836

DIVERSION OF 1852

RIVER

CABLE INCLINE

PASSENGER GOODS

ORIGINAL ROUTE

0 50·YARDS·100 150

102. Propelling the wagons past Old Dinas Junction entertained the children of the area on 28th July 1956. The site of the old main line to Dinas (above the locomotive) has been obliterated by the tip. The gateway on the left once accommodated the line to Nidd-y-Gigfram Quarry. (A.M.Davies)

BLAENAU FFESTINIOG

103.   In the background is the FR station at which passengers alighted to connect with trains to Llandudno. In the foreground is evidence of the track removal mentioned in caption 78. The date is 15th March 1956. (A.G.W.Garraway)

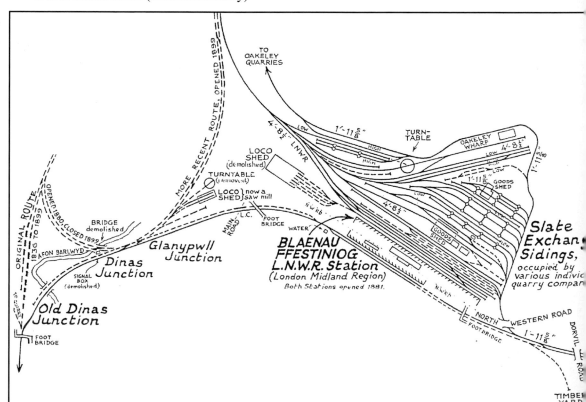

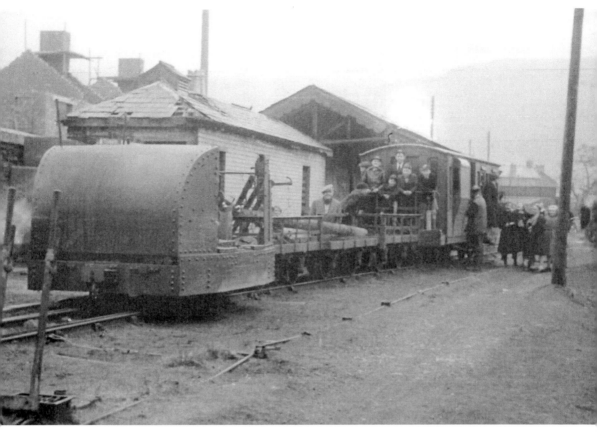

104.   Fred Boughey and Allan Garraway took their families to Blaenau Ffestiniog on 9th April 1956 to collect a telephone pole wanted for reuse. As always, the local lads arrived like bees round a honey pot. The new BR station is nearing completion in the background. (F.Boughey)

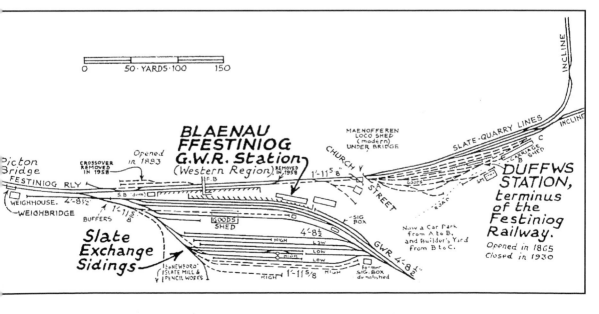

105.   Track clearance was required at the former GWR station before the first train could be shunted. Trains from Bala still used the platform on the left. Following the decline of the slate industry, the population of Blaenau Ffestiniog diminished from 9078 in 1931 to 6920 in 1951. (A.G.W.Garraway)

106.   This and the previous picture were taken on 5th March 1955 on the site of the present BR platform. The Simplex is ready to return with coach no. 17 and van no. 1, the first FR train here since 1946. (A.G.W.Garraway)

107.   At Blaenau Ffestiniog some of the quarry companies continued to use the FR to take their slates to the ex LMS and GWR sidings. The Oakeley Company's diesel wagons, and stacks of slates are seen in the LMS yard on 12th September 1958. (J.L.Alexander)

108. Another view of the Oakeley diesel shows it pulling wagons under the bridge from the ex-LMS yard on the same day. In addition to rent from its cottages, the FR derived an income from leasing this part of the line from the closure until the 1960s. (J.L.Alexander)

109.   The ex-GWR headshunt was crossed by the narrow gauge, though in later years it was stopped off by a sleeper stop block, to prevent BR trains using it. The footbridge in this 1953 picture has been seen earlier in picture no. 105. (A.M.Davies)

110.   The exchange sidings in the former GWR yard were in use throughout the 1950s. The goods shed is in the background of the previous picture. The crane (left) was of 6-ton capacity. This is now the site of a school. (J.L.Alexander)

111.   The FR Duffws terminal buildings are behind the wall that was erected after the cessation of passenger services here on 31st December 1931. The Oakeley diesel is propelling wagons to the foot of the incline on 6th July 1950. (A.M.Davies)

112.   Turning round, albeit three years later, we see the incline to the Votty & Bowydd Quarry. The lines on the left led to an incline which conveyed slates from the Maenofferen and Rhiwbach Quarries, the latter being about two miles distant. (A.M.Davies)

113.   Rhiwbach Quarry was in use until 1953, its output being hauled by horses along the
Rhiwbach Tramway and into the Maenofferen system. Wagons descended two inclines before
reaching the one mentioned in the previous caption. The disused tramway is seen beside Llyn
Bowydd in August 1956. (A.M.Davies)

5. Off Line Recovery
WAENFAWR

114.   The body of ex-WHR no. 26, a sister coach to no. 23, still existed as a hen house at Waenfawr. It was purchased and moved to the railway, being put on bogies from no. 21, which had stood outside at Boston Lodge and was considered beyond economic repair. (A.G.W.Garraway)

115.   The move took place on 26th October 1958, using an ex-Army Bedford. The wheel chock indicates that the hand brake was in doubt. The trailer had none, although a hose pipe was in place to give a contrary impression. MOT testing was still in the future. (A.G.W.Garraway)

CROESOR

116.   Three useful iron wagons of the Croesor Quarries still existed near Croesor village and were kindly donated by them. These were collected on 15th November 1958 and were very useful for ashes. (A.G.W.Garraway)

117.   A few lengths of WHR track had never been lifted due to flooding where it passed under the road at Pitt's Head. These rails were recovered in an Operation known as "Garraway's bath" and were used to replace badly corroded ones on the Cob, which were given to the receivers of the WHR in exchange. The date is 15th November 1958. (A.G.W.Garraway)

SNAPPER

118.   One of the biggest recovery operations in railway preservation in the 1950s was that of the Lynton & Barnstaple Railway coach at Snapper, Devon. It was standing complete on two lengths of the track. As it would not fit under FR bridges, two people spent a week carefully dismantling the body into sections that could easily be handled. (A.G.W.Garraway)

119.   Most body parts of no. 6993 were loaded on 25th and 26th April 1959, leaving the bogies on the track on which they had run until 1935. (A.G.W.Garraway)

120.   The underframe and bogies left Devon on 3rd May 1959 but it was to be 1963 before the coach ran on the FR, as no. 14. Details of this fascinating but less fortunate railway can be seen in the Middleton Press album *Branch Line to Lynton*. The coach was rebuilt to the new enlarged FR loading gauge to which all subsequent stock has been constructed. This is only one example of the improvements initiated in the 1950s that were to lead to the FR becoming world famous once again. (N.F.Gurley)

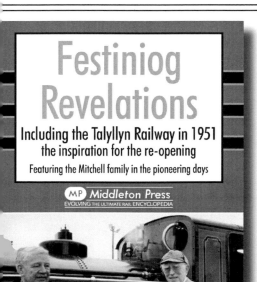

MP Middleton Press

Easebourne Lane, Midhurst, West Sussex.
GU29 9AZ Tel:01730 813169

www.middletonpress.co.uk email:info@middletonpress.co.uk

A-978 0 906520 B- 978 1 873793 C- 978 1 901706 D-978 1 904474
E - 978 1 906008 F - 978 1 908174

EVOLVING THE ULTIMATE RAIL ENCYCLOPEDIA

All titles listed below were in print at time of publication - please check current availability by looking at our website - *www.middletonpress.co.uk* or by requesting a Brochure which includes our *LATEST* RAILWAY TITLES also our TRAMWAY, TROLLEYBUS, MILITARY and COASTAL series